Steam in South Africa

A Photographic Odyssey

Compiled by Ron White

TOTEM

PUBLISHING

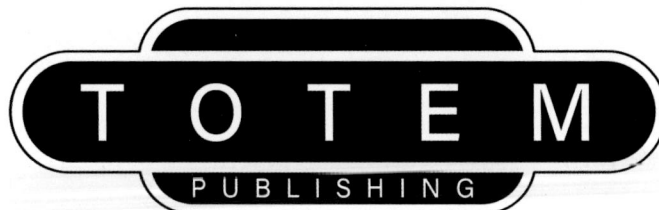

© Images and design: The Transport Treasury 2020. Text Ron White

ISBN 978-1-913893-02-6

First Published in 2020 by Transport Treasury Publishing Ltd. 16 Highworth Close, High Wycombe, HP13 7PJ

Totem Publishing, an imprint of Transport Treasury Publishing.

www.ttpublishing.co.uk

Printed in the UK by Short Run Press Ltd. Exeter.

*'Steam in South Africa' is one of a series of books on specialist transport subjects published in strictly limited numbers
and produced under the Totem Publishing imprint using material only available at The Transport Treasury.*

Front Cover: I4CRM 1762 leaves Sir Lowry's Pass station for the summit; her tiny driving wheels are made for hill-climbing - and what a backdrop; the wonderfully named Hottentots Holland range. 6 April 1971.

Frontispiece: 1. How rarely do we see a shot of the station area at Cape Town; here is 3R 1448 shunting stock with Table Mountain as a bonus. We'd all gone to wherever (after Paarden Eiland shed). 8 April 1971.

Rear cover: I could only use a beautiful picture as a final tribute to a good man and fine photographer and generous contributor when I ran Colour-Rail all those years ago. All I know is that it is shot 29 on reel 415 taken in October 1973 in the Bloemfontein area; I can see it's a 15F and almost certainly coming in to Bloemfontein on the line from Springfontein. The leading vehicle is an old "refrigerated" van - they had water tanks on the roof and hollow walls filled with coke (?) and the water trickled through and evaporated and kept the contents cool. Then three old carriages and a guard's van but where has it come from? Somewhere with freight, possibly with people though that is less likely - just another unanswered question but what fun it has been to go through these precious slides and put a story together. Oh, and don't overlook that these pictures are what he took on the cameras of the time; they haven't been photoshopped to death, what you see is what he got and you can't say that of most of what gets printed today!

Steam in South Africa   A Photographic Survey

Ron White – wasn't he somebody once? Wasn't he the man who was Colour-Rail, sold millions of slides and was disrespectful to Great Western lovers? Can't be him, surely he's not still around and capable of doing anything - must be someone with the same name. But no, it is me, rising 89 and delighted to have been asked to do this for the Transport Treasury. One had bought a few of their books and knew Barry Hoper from years back, got talking to the new owner who lived close by, found we had much in common save age and he had collections of slides, many of which were before his time, plus others he wanted to use in books. One of these was Peter Gray's overseas collection, in particular South Africa where I had made many trips and could identify many anonymous slides for him. Peter had been a contributor to Colour-Rail from 1980 supplying much of the BRW section of the catalogue, but the slides were always his choice and, considering some of my crisp comments on HIS railway, I was lucky to get as much as I did. To make geographical sense of the two visits I've used them in reverse order, going from the Cape to Johannesburg in 1971, then from Pretoria to Empangeni and beyond in 1967. In many ways, this is an apologia to him, a tribute to a genuine, reserved, gentle man, who in 1967, when most of us were flogging knackered Black 5s round Lancashire, he was away, HIS railway had gone but there were riches abroad; it took most of us years to catch up: well done mate!

Ron White, Chesham, Bucks., August 2020

2. I OCR pacific 777 pauses at Vishoek on her way back from Simonstown with the daily freight, about the last line job for these lovely little Pacifics.
7 April 1971.

3. 19C 2456 TAKBOK has received a spark arresting arrangement of astounding ugliness and unknown efficiency; this was devised by the shed master at Paarden Eiland after wheat fields in the Western Cape had been incinerated. Seen at Malmesbury. 7 April 1971.

4. 19C 2449 leaving the station for the summit of Sir Lowry's Pass with freight for Steenbras. 6 April 1971.

5. GEA 4002 lifts a load of empties towards the summit at the classic spot where so many photographers gave up the chase not knowing what delights lay ahead, too many of us thought quantity first. 6 April 1971.

6. The little sub-shed at Caledon is bulging with GEA Garratts and 19Cs; the Garratts will just manage the 1975 apple crop though by then on their last legs (if Garratts have legs). 6 April 1971.

(Left) 7. A year or two ago disparaging comments were written (by Australians would you believe?) about the "habitually ill-washed English" who never got east of Sir Lowry's Pass. Peter certainly did and these two exquisite shots of 19C 2460 shunting at Caledon are proof.
9 April 1971.

(Right) 8. Trying to make a choice, I couldn't bear to pass over either and so you shall enjoy them both as well. 2460 again across the water. 9 April 1971.

(Left) 9. Peter didn't find the second horror-comic GEA 4009 RENOSTER here seen at Caledon in 1969. Dusty Durrant wrote that sparks were expected to die of fright as they bounced along the long dark pipes. (Ron White collection)

(Above) 10. GEA 4032 leaves Elgin with a full load for Cape Town, a stiff climb at 1 in 40 (or worse) round the lake (reservoir?). 6 April 1971.

(Above) 11. This climb could (and did) demand assistance and the GEA is happy to take a push from l4CRB 1767, the Elgin pilot. 6 April 1971.

(Right) 12. Peter had intended to cover the Ladysmith branch to get the lovely old 7th class 4-8-0 but it wasn't the day the branch ran and so he made a quick detour to Touws River shed where 7A 101 I awaited his pleasure, what elegance! This was where they built a coaling plant as the line was being wired; geniuses everywhere. 6 April 1971.

(Above) 13. 6B 500 looks a bit wan at Worcester, but there is fire in her belly and she is station/shed pilot. SAR could keep them going on jobs such as this and Peter benefitted. 8 April 1971.

(Right) 14. Peter then followed the Garden Route eastwards and at Drew found a gleaming GMAM 41 16 on a Worcester - Riversdale freight. 9 April 1971.

15. 3BR 1458 is still in a fine state of cleanliness at Voorbaai shed - the class kept their original flared chimneys to the end; and were spared the stovepipe so many classes endured. 11 April 1971.

16. We must have one shot on the Montagu Pass even though the fickle weather was unkind; gleaming GEA 4039 brings freight to Topping. 11 April 1971.

(Left) 17. The Oudtshoorn pilot was a very vigorous 8C 1 190, the 24s hadn't arrived by then so did she cover the Calitzdorp branch as well. 11 April 1971.

(Above) 18. l9D 3339 in the depths of Toorwaterpoort. Peter eschewed the wide view from across the river to get the claustrophobic feel of that narrow slot in the mountains. 11 April 1971.

19. Decision time - follow the main line via Klipplaat or go direct for RE? Go direct was the answer and follow the narrow gauge which he picked up east of Loerie at Summit where NGG16 82 appeared with limestone for RE. 13 April 1971.

20. Waiting in the loop was NGG 15 1 17, so both types of loco were covered with a minimum of effort. We little knew that NGG 16s would form a part of the Welsh narrow gauge 40 years later! 13 April 1971.

21. Van Stadens Bridge has to be included and this angle emphasises the height of it if not the length - the gauge is 2' 0" not HO. NGG 15 122 pedals happily westwards.
13 April 1971.

22. Humewood Road was the narrow gauge shed in Port Elizabeth and contained a few relics as well as the running stock. NGG 1 1 55 was one of a pair still then on the shunt and 54 is still around today all tarted up for the tourists.
13 April 1971.

23. The approach to the terminus at RE was made hideous by flyovers and it was hard to do justice to 16CR pacific 839 coming in from Uitenhage with a suburban set arriving at 08.13 and packed solid. She has been given a stovepipe chimney, shame. 13 April 1971.

24. The docks shunt was a major part of the business and no better loco could be found than the classic class I I 929 - the only 2-8-2s on the 3 foot 6 inch system. They only had a couple of years to live, but, once withdrawn, industry stepped in and bought them and they lasted for years and were loved by their new owners. 13 April 1971.

25. Something Peter didn't see on his visit was this l5F with yet another smoke deflecting arrangement - a batch of these was allocated to Sydenham for working the line to Rosmead via Cradock where some were sub-shedded to work through the tight tunnels. The arms were swung up over a cut-down chimney and the exhaust was diverted downwards and sideways which must have been fun for the crews. The poor devils at Wellingborough who had fought with the Crosti-boilered 9Fs would have sympathised. (1968 Ron White collection)

26. Sydenham shed was always seething with locomotives,(I5ARs/ 16CRs/24s) but here we have an interesting survivor, pacific 749 of class IOBR, which must have been one of the last to run the Uitenhage service before the 16CRs arrived. 14 April 1971.

(Left) 27. 16CR 800 (named Uitenhage, you can see the cast name plate above the handrail) has the 09.45 Uitenhage to RE. These trains were scheduled very tightly and it was common for crews to get up to 100 kph between stops; and many drivers would not touch the brakes until they were between the platforms at stations! 14 April 1971.

(Above) 28. Going the other way, 16CR 808 near Redhouse with the 12.55 RE -Uitenhage - this was even harder work uphill, both locos still have the flared chimneys which made such a difference. 13 April 1971.

(Above) 29. It was a long slog from RE to Klipplaat but the 15ARs took it in their stride, even if the tender was pretty empty on arrival; at Kleinpoort with still a couple of hours to go, 15AR 1807 leaves after crossing one going to RE. This was another line few people covered, it wasn't very scenic, just hard work. 14 April 1971.

(Right) 30. Peter went on to the Lootsberg (as we all did, eventually) and not only did he collect a bunch of pictures but a positively Old Testamentary swarm of locusts amongst which he sat until l9B 1407 appeared with freight. 15 April 1971.

(Left) 31. There are few views of trains descending the upper part of the bank but here is I9B 1409 on the pick-up from which she will come off at Bethesda Road, turn on the triangle and swap trains with the up one. How splendidly sinuous are the curves and what a drag on the return job for these short valve travel, raucous, loveable hill-climbers. 15 April 1971.

(Above) 32. 1409 returns with the pick-up from Graaff Reinet; a fullish load today, ten bogies and a brake must be close to the limit. 15 April 1971.

33. Having failed to be eaten by the swarm Peter moved on to Jagpoort where all southbound trains stopped for fire-cleaning and to take water and the pilot (if double-headed) went to the rear and banked the train to the summit where it quietly dropped off and turned on the triangle, and returned to Rosmead. Peter was lucky to get the solitary 19BR 1410 on the point (as the Americans say and I wish they wouldn't). 15 April 1971.

34. 19B 1402 gives a healthy shove-up to the summit; even if the gates were across the road, there was time enough to get ahead. 15 April 1971.

(Left) 35. Traversing that lovely curve, 19Bs 1413/1407 have the Mossel Bay - Johannesburg in full cry; in those days some Rosmead drivers FIRED the locos from Blouwater to the summit and the firemen drove (or collapsed on his seat for a while). Peter went back for the passenger which was northbound on Tuesdays and Fridays only, and yesterday's UFOs had hoovered up what little there had been and gone. 16 April 1971.

(Above) 36. On to De Aar where the station pilot was unusually a glittering 12AR 21 12 CINDY; MILLY must be having a rest (or up the coal stage,THAT was a full time job at that busy shed full of 25 NCs and condensers with healthy appetites). 21 April 1971.

37. Even rarer was 15BR 1979, which he found on another, undated visit; possibly a candidate for the museum collection that the shed master had built up over the years but which did not survive intact.

38. North to Kimberley, collecting class 23 2565 WILLEMIEN somewhere along the way north of Orange River. October 1973.

39. As the evening light warms up, 25NC 3424 leads 23 2565 WILLEMIEN southbound through Graspan, odd how he should find the same 23 class loco, same driver, same girlfriend two years apart. 20 April 1971.

40. Spotless 25NC 3446 carries the Orange Express headboard as it comes through Beaconsfield where some catenary existed to allow freight from the Warrenton line directly to the yards. 20 April1971.

41. Another 25NC carries the headboard on Beaconsfield shed; this is 3468, the second one to be decondensed, and the tender has an odd little deck at the rear which can just be seen, the only one thus fitted - 3452, the first one, had by far the best looking tender and it was a great pity the rest were defiled for reasons of cost and weight. October 1973.

42. Bloemfontein could be approached from all four points of the compass; we'll leave Kimberley and go back to Noupoort where there was a shed (Midlandia) and the line north had not been dieselised. 12R 1943 is a good solid lump to be on the shunt. 16 April 1971.

43. North of Noupoort a good road followed the line and pacing shots (for cine) could be got; Peter simply went for a perfect broadside of 23 class 3264 on the Mossel Bay - Pretoria - many of us thought these were the best proportioned of all the 4-8-2s. 16 April 1971.

44. Night photography? Nothing to it - 16E pacific 858 ALLAN G. WATSON sleeps the night away in Springfontein shed. A classic loco and a technically perfect picture. 16 April 1971.

(Above) 45. Fauresmith? Been there, done that, but not with a shiny class 24 No.3658 and a load to fill the street. In 1974 on our first trip I got a scruffy 19D on a van and two coaches, then went and bought some Tiger Oats in the shop to bring home, got back to the car and found my mate flaked out dehydrated and had to get him to Bloemfontein to recover (which he did by laying in bed in the hotel drinking water and tape recording: very therapeutic). Memories, memories. 15 April 1971.

(Right) 46. The Orange River is crossed and the bridge is in the background as 16E pacific 855 has the northbound pick-up. 6'0" drivers and poppet valves would not be ideal but she must work out her mileage somehow. 17 April 1971.

(Above) 47. We move up to Pauling and here's another one, 857 on a southbound freight, pictures of these working are rare. 17 April 1971.

(Right) 48. Class 23 3268 with the Mossel Bay - Pretoria at Rietwater (wherever that may be) on the run in to Bloemfontein in lovely evening light; this is why we went (eventually). Don't get fed up with the 23s; they haven't got long to live but were still the favourite engines of those days at Bloemfontein (and Kroonstad!). 19 April 1971.

49. A couple of shots on the western exit from Bloemfontein to Kimberley, a curve designed for photographers. Class 23 3291 has the Orange Express but not the headboard. 20 April 1971.

50. The curve was generous enough to allow double-headed condensers with their massive tenders to be included; class 25 Nos. 3455 and 3460 whine away westwards. 20 April 1971.

51. Bloemfontein shed was always bustling with locos coming on and off their trains, and the residents waking from sleep and blowing down their boilers before starting work. 19 April 1971.

52. The works was equally busy and vast - it could do most things and did and is still being helpful to the Sandstone Railway today. October 1973.

53. Karee could not be ignored by any photographer, no better or busier place for steam in Africa with up to 120 trains up and down the hill. The wires came in 1974 and spoiled it, by 1973 the 23s had nearly finished so it was a diet of 15Fs, in pairs or singly, take your pick. Peter took no numbers, and I can't read them. October 1973.

54. Skating downhill, little more work to be done today. October 1973.

(Above) 55. Peter went by train to Kroonstad, who burnished their 23s, and at Dorenkoms found his only 15E of the trip, 2870 on a southbound freight - these were supposed to be around in 1971 but weren't. Just a grab shot out of the window but how valuable. 22 April 1971.

(Right) 56. Handsome 16DA pacific 850 has the 07.10 to Melorane on the Bethlehem line, a sort of commuter service which would have been a 10 BR a year or two earlier. This loco suffered the indignity of being stuffed and mounted on a road roundabout outside Theunissen. 20 April 1971.

57. Leaky 19C 2442 on the 08.00 Bloemfontein - Ladybrand at Kerelaw, another station on the outskirts of the city. 20 April 1971.

58. In 1972 Ian Allan issued "Steam on the Veld" and the dust jacket picture of a 15F and 15E departing simultaneously from Bloemfontein made me (and many others) decide we MUST go and have some of that! Peter had already been, but only got 15F 3012 going to Bethlehem; that cover picture had been fixed by Charlie Lewis who worked for SAR/SAS and could (and did) do things. 20 April 1971.

59. Despite their alleged availability in 1971, the 15Es, which had nearly monopolised the Bethlehem line, simply weren't working, and we have to go back to 1969 to get No. 2880 on the same working but without the parallel working to Springfontein. (Ron White collection)

60. Peter followed the line to Bethlehem under grey skies and with nothing but 15Fs on all trains but he did find the shed pilot, lovely 60. 6J 641, waiting for him. This had been another of Charlie's bright ideas; in September 1969, 641 and an equally surprised 8A 1 104 were bulled up and sent out on a freight to Frankfort after years of doing nothing. This wheeze produced some of the loveliest pictures I've ever seen (sadly, Peter wasn't there) but near Reitz 641 bent her right hand leading crankpin and was a total failure. Scrap her, surely? More fixing by Charlie; into works, and the shed master got his pet back as good as new. 23 April 1971.

61. (Left) His trip ended, as most did, waiting all day for the evening flight home from Johannesburg; so, go and bash the sheds and yards. Krugersdorp yielded GM Garratt 2297 of that tiny class then working to Mafeking via Zeerust. 25 April 1971.

62. (Bottom) Even scarcer was 4AR 1557, all ten of which were based here and did little line work; 1554 went to de Aar for Alec Watson's potential museum collection, but did it survive? 25 April 1971.

63. (Right) Braamfontein yards demanded heavy shunters and did they get some! Monstrous SI 3802 of the second batch (from NBL) crushes the rails; the first batch of ten of these hairy-chested beasts were the only locos ever built direct by SAR at Salt River works. 25 April 1971.

64. Peter's first trip started in the north and covered some lines which very soon went diesel or electric, so, swiftly off to Lydenburg where the shed pilot was a dignified class IA No. 1291, and the shed was of surprising size to cope with the Steelpoort traffic. 10 July 1967.

65. Up early, as the rowdy GO Garratts went about their business, one has already taken the passenger to Pretoria, now at 09.00 2579 blisters off to Steelpoort. How strange that SAR could find jobs for all other classes once their line was finished with steam, but these virile beasts got dumped at de Aar and rotted away. 1 July 1967.

66. (Above) Off to Waterval Boven, where the coal stage pilot was class 6 No.432. The fireman is crackling with enthusiasm, and the driver on the far side appears to be asleep, not a place for sleepwalkers. 11 July 1967.

67. (Right) The Nelspruit - Graskop line was the preserve of the GF Garratts and here is 2431 somewhere on the line. Pretty little things and wonderfully popular when they were withdrawn; the Enyati Railway was full of them. 10 July 1967.

68. (Above) Not another GMAM? Not quite; look at the chimney. What chimney? Not a lot, it's been ground down and is but an inch tall so that smoke deflecting shields could be fitted like those fitted to the 15F at Sydenham in picture 25. Only the base remains; I didn't know a few "Gammatts" (so called by their crews) got that treatment but I do remember seeing others with a pimple of a chimney and wondering why - I' ve never seen a list of numbers (can any reader help?) but know of three, 4052/4057/4142. 4052 is here at Sewefontein working down to Breyten. 11 July 1967.

69. (Right) Trees! Shade! Carolina with a classic 15AR No. 1848 on the shunt. 11 July 1967.

70. (Left) Class I 1248 is shed pilot at Breyten , nobody seemed interested in the line to Lothair until years later. 11 July 1967.

71. (Bottom) One of Peter's anonymous ones; from the slide number we know it has to be between Breyten and Dundee; it is a tiny GCA Garratt, and was taken on 11 July 1967 but WHERE? Probably going to one of the many collieries in that area.

72. (Right) From one of the smallest to quite definitely the largest GL Garratt; 2351 PRINCESS ALICE has just arrived at the shed at Glencoe. 13 July 1967.

73. The shed pilot at Glencoe in those days was this charming 8DW No 1248, a rare survivor.13 July 1967.

74. On down to Durban (why did he miss Pietermaritzburg?) where the dock area was alive with steam, too many 14Rs of which this is one, number unrecorded, at Point. 16 July 1967.

75. The only tank engines to be found were these H2 class 4-8-2Ts which were originally built as 4-10-2Ts and this clearly shows the gap where the rear axle was removed, at Wests. 16 July 1967.

76. From ancient to modern, the final design of shunter which gave the builders Krupp a few headaches to comply with the SAR specification. S2 0-8-0 3778 at Wests. 16 July 1967.

77. (Left) Moving to Greyville freight is being handled, inevitably by a 14R but piloted by a 15CA, variety at last.
16 July 1967.

78. (Top) Yes, those ancient tanks took their full part on the shunt; H2 259 shows her well-ventilated cab as she happily bashes wagons at Greyville.
16 July 1967.

79. (Bottom) Peter suddenly appears at Empangeni far up the coast and produces this shot of a GE Garratt 2265 on shed; but in the collection this was preceded by aerial views over the town and over Richards Bay (taken through the canopy; they cannot be used) and a shot of a Piper Tripacer on the airfield at Empangeni - was this a joyride or did he come all the way up from Durban in it? Just another question that will never be answered.
18 July 1967.

80. Stanger shed provided GDA Garratt 2256; useful little things for the sugar cane traffic. 17 July 1967.

81. I5CB 2065 is potent power for the 09.30 Stanger/Empangeni/ Durban passenger, loud and exuberant they were. 17 July 1967.

82. Down in the forest, something stirred - it was only the note of a - Class 19A 1368 on her way to one of the paper mills which abounded along the North Coast. 18 July 1967.